lilac

ARVINA KORI

Writer's Pocket

First published by Writer's Pocket in 2023

email: publish@writerspocket.com

cover design by Radha Tole

ISBN-13: 978-93-6083-152-3

www.writerspocket.com

to all the lilacs yearning to be seen and heard!

1. I'd like to thank to those dark nights to make me write my thoughts and feel it.
2. A heartfelt appreciation to the lilac of my life, the true muse behind my love poems.
3. And all those pretty dark spots upon Moon, which inspires me to accept my flaws and shine when it's time.

I meow you!
Arvina Kori - arko

lady to the shop

what lingers cult,
yet shakes our extant sight?
i fret, embrace my dwelling's arch.
i shall forge a haven, anew,
alike the one i bade adieu.

a furniture embodied the fortitude of a home,
i'd sever the mightiest,
lest it crumble never.

what actually shatters the "home" in decay?
how would i discern?
as i always witness, the disarray.

a prowess,
she always prepared a feast,
i am ought to delect,
the tastiest fruit from the shop.

in the marketplace's realm,
i may procure all,
to recreate the home i departed,
i might find everything from the shop.

sweet william

a world captive in its own maladies,
shackled by ill decree.
but dear sweet william,
you chose to be unhinged,
unbound by stale constraints.

but,
sweet william,
when our difference bars us from their standard
norm,
labeled as impure and forlorn.
a world that cannot fathom the awe of existence,
they call us sick and absurd.

you can grace with tattered clothes,
and smoky eyes that mystifies,
you can put million layers of disguise,
and the authentic grace,
a pink shade, like a mermaid empress.

an orchid field across the end town

she went to the green field,
fierce enough to be a sinner,

she clasped her soft sigh,
supple and quivering lips,
the field, turning in wet pink,
as an orchid blooms solely for her beloved.

she swept her fingertips over her beloved,
clutched her hand,
about to vanish,
wandering the calmness.

like the sky erupts,
a destruction is seen.
like a holy castle,
holds an invisible sin.

the pink petals whirling into burnt amber,
untouched yet buried down.
the garden makes no sound,
but a faded souvenir of seira and iris.

blacksmith's cottage

the rigid barriers of horizons,
the iron rust,
severing its own warm essence.

his foe in a teary-rainfall,
wiping away the weeping-n-grief.
dimming of the light,
like, a pretentious attempt,
to call out the rust.

each night,
he lights up the candle,
with hope to to melt down,
these walls, made out of its own.

he hides himself, being the decay,
cause the illness, ill-ing to hale.

"dear mother",

you mislead me in this
deluded universe,
those courteous thoughts
and warmth words.

you drove me to dwell
in this brutal rabble.
i snipped the bullet when
only trained to break a pebble.

i sobbed all night long,
and shone brightly
in the sunlight.

the world is harrowing,
the world is cruel,

where is the kindness?
perhaps the world was always rude.

you would not allow to me to go through this,
it's a defeat, defeat in million pieces,
i failed as a child,
you were right, i was my father's daughter,
but never, a mother's child.

with every sunset,
my world crumbles down.
and with each sunrise,
i stapled metals in the borrowed crown.

i was tied with this shiny crown,
so were those lies to my soul.

i long for peace,
but i only know,
how to end things?

they cut me in the half,
but i bled in glitter.

but we are no saint,
in the world of sinners.

no, you didn't teach me but,
here everything is a mirror.

knife or swords never kills,
they killed me
with silly word pills.

you said soul splits up at the dusk,
how would i know?

my soul left me,
even before the sun was at its peak.

dear mother,

i long
for peace,
but
i only
know,
how to end things?

celebrating grief

the new year clinging upon the door,
the grief still holding me in its arms,
a loneliness that hanging to me like a shroud,
engraving me with a cold battle.

the laughter and greetings,
i want to hear it for the last time,
these masses stifling me with their fists,
wondering if i was a person, to be cared.

the lights swinging, barely shining,
some gone for good,
some curled up in fuss,
i might unthread it for better.

the new year clinging upon the door,
the abyss days making me numb,
i wonder if solitude is what i always do.

i do, i am,
i long for the affection,
but it seems to reject me at every turn.

i am drowning in the adrifting ocean of alienation,
the ocean called, 'a tunnel to heaven',
i try to swim through the misty blue,
searching for a passage to sucked onto.

i celebrate grief,
like i was taught to live through it.

“Do you accept death?” The death angel Ronin asked Zoa.
“Does my desire hold any significance? what if i were to deny!”.

“I am still young, I have not beheld the exquisiteness of skies. I have not spoken to my mother the words that i love her. I didn’t brew the coffee that my uncle always brought from the south. I have not tasted the oldest wine yet. I carry with me the baggage of responsibility for my family’s sake. I have not kissed the darl girl I know. Indeed, there are moments when I wish not to wake up, but before sleeping I beseech the rugs to rouse me before the sun. I never cherished the rain that trickled through the roof and poured into my downy palm, making the sublime dripping tone. I did not pluck the flowers simply for the joy of their bloom. I have yet to live, yet to breathe. I do not wanna perish!”

"May god forgive your transgressions, your reluctant sins!,

But in the realm of birth and death, one cannot flee death; a man born therein is destined for mortality, one must become an integral part of the eternal cycle."
He took his hand, like a reaper takes its tastiest prey for feed.

to the july

to the july,
where nothing beautiful happens,
and time simply slips away.

to the july where i encounter naught,
but a mystic sense of emptiness.
the month that showers infinite raindrops,
just so i can cover mine.

the ocean doesn't blush but leaves a horror of passing.
the moon hides behind the shattered ego of its loneliness.

july where the leaves do not descend the way i cherish,
the flowers don't seem to be the kind of tangerine i like.
when the roads don't shine,
but leaves a void that i avoid.

tell me if it is what it is,
july taught me that sometimes you are merely an existence.

where nothing magical happens.
you don't fall in love, you don't fall out.
you are not the main character anymore,

what makes it crueler?
the months surrounded in beauty.
and it chose to be the dark spot,
that one wishes to go away with time.

i shall wait until the august emerges,
and i may start breathing the air again,
an air infused with the desire to embrace life,
rediscovering the enchantment again.

yet, life does not solely revolve around waiting for others,
but embrace what you love,
and stick with it. right?

an ugly bloodline

a corrupted brew, flowing through the veins,
long have i been tainted through and through.
deeper the stain i put, it lingers still,
a lineage i could never overbrim.

the art of greater child,
though i may falter, and run unruly, wild.

i stumble,
call me a stumbler.

amidst the fields of blooming lilac flair,
i am colored red, a spare like none to care.

they tended the lilac with tender braid,
a red stood neglected, a burden to bear.
a discarded seed,
in between left to wither.

a lineage, hideous as scar,
one that many would cut to avoid by far,
a cursed tree, sacrilege wind,
a branch that many flee.

one nurtured bright bloom,
an ugly bloodline robbed,
barely becoming a child,
a tainted wild.

---

in the dark forest i roam,
seeking out a green shadow, a place to call home.
everything i grasp,
reaches for nothing.

the moon lurking in haze that's gray,
the cursed ray, to the earthy bay,
it pours the rain so called,
even in hate, i plead for even more.

my mother taught me to love,
but never being loved.

my father taught me to helm the hunt,
hunting me later.

lilac

attraction

she in the brown dress
with a restless gaze
and ocean-like eyes.
she sat by the window seat,
of that cafe-house,
held that book,
with a heavy sigh.

and the uncurled dark hair,
covering the brown eyes.
brawling through the swirling air!

"ohh, are you the one,
they talk about?
or it's just a wish,
to get seen by you!".

and my thoughts persevered!
how does her morning coffee
tastes like?

when the sun doesn't shine well!
does she make it go right,
or just sips it away?

what kind of music band
does she like?
or she lives within
the poet's dead ink?

is she as enlightened by the
sunset as i am?
or the moon bringing,
void in a blink?

does she feels the urge to,
smell the old books?
or it smells just like her!
all lilac and peachy!

searching the book
for her existence,
ohh, she tried to be a good guy,
in everyone's life!
does she keep her apartment

all tidy and neat,
or she is the mess,
trying to clean it all day bleak.

what color does she live in?
is it lilac or white?
like the snow.
or beige, like she dress?

they say their eyes speak,
when they can't explain a thing.
but i guess i never knew
a thing to speak.

does she love being at home in fall?
or here, in shiny spring!
or she lives in all, live it all?

like i keep my secrets in my poems,
does she keep it in her art?
or she swallows it all,
being no one at all!
nothing at all!!

she in the sage dress
with restless gaze,
and ocean-like eyes!

lilac

attachment

across the dark room,
with artificial lights on,
bursting with smiles
but she, the splendid one.

the curvy-n-slender grin,
might rip the heart of 'em
a glimpse at that artistry,
could never be a sin.

"hey",
the little flutter of hers,
carved a piece to heart-of-mine,

"ohh hey",
"wish we met earlier"
- my heart throbbing with no echo.
- but it stayed just within me.

that bright green,

that lights screeching on her face.

who could be that enticing?

a daydream,

- or a poets writhing.

lilac

love

she in lilac, snatching away my soul at her,
the giggle still lingering in my head.
i don't yearn, but it's really her,
making me fall even harder.

a warmest fall, leaves showering in chronic,
but she enticing me, all. all at once.
does she realize the affection she had on me?
like a dandelion longs for wishes to come close.

like a warm head waits for the downpour,
i would stay-n-abide to,
only to be the beholder of her gaze.
i beseech her, gush every ounce of it.

i will long for it,
like a sunflower waits for the sun to rise.

ohh, to love her!

to be lilac!

to love lilac!

lilac

peace

and the april sung in spring petals,
a chorus of colors in choir of glitter,
but she, in midsummer,
was like, rain on heavy chatter.

her eyes speak the language of heaven,
i want to be the holy ambassador,
my dear, the world threatens,
but she shines with ample metal.

like a nightingale of a fiery night,
raises a flame that ignites.
a scarlet twill, like a petty steal,
i wander, but red is hard to conceal.

she in the crimson red dress,
with a restless gaze,
and ocean-like eyes.

---

kill me with a knife, i might bleed.
kill me with love, i might live.

why i stop eating oranges?

i woke up in the misty weather,
it's a lazy sunday, as my will to live.
maybe i will brew some coffee,
with beans stored in the lower drawer.

i will draw the drapes,
the darkness soothes my soul.
maybe i will play a country music,
and imagine myself in it.

it's 2 o'clock and i am still on the bed,
peeking out of the window.
the cold air blowing through,
the little hole from the window.

there are oranges stored in refrigerator,
that i bought days ago,
maybe i will peel some,
i forgot why i always liked oranges,
now i rarely eat it, maybe i will blend some.

maybe i will bake a cake,
i won't burn bottom this time.
maybe i will go and meet my friends at arc,
but i am still in my house.

maybe i will take a cold bath,
and put some lipstick for validation.
maybe i will tick off all my to-do from list.
feels like the blankets have swollen me.

maybe i will do my nails,
and put the fancy polish,
that i bought months ago.

maybe i will iron those,
oversized shirts that i bought from the male
section,
maybe i will wear other colors,
rather than black and darker shades.

i spent my hours before screen,
to put a perfect eye liner.
today, i will drink enough water.
maybe i will live a little.

maybe i will be a little less messy,
i will put my blankets in place.
change pillow to light red covers,

it's midnight, the bed has never been different.

burnt child

i was a child with a flammable skin,
i let them burn the piece of mine.
i adore fire as if i were born from it.
after all, my father named me - *a burnt child.*

i hid behind the walls,
built from my own toxins,
bricked with darker shades of mine.

each day i burn a part of it,
shredding the walls.

i set the lantern with an orange blaze,
as my father said,
you can't burn a house,
without burning yourself.
guess i never let him down.

what it takes to be loved by all,
all i know is, no one loves
a fire in their dorm.

i carry the flame as i breath the void,
i fear the spark couldn't be damned,
a burnt child is never burnt alone.
they scorch down the dead with my ablaze,
i was the last thing,
they could get in their veins.
after all, my father named me - *a burnt child.*

they blame child for the burnt house,
little did they know,
it was already burning for a while.

the squirrel and the death angel ronin

My mother claimed to have witnessed some of history's worst nights. Darker enough to vanish and leave no footprint in its trail. My mother told me that in order to protect the land, we must all perish. The earth has suffered a lot. We, a species with no worth in other life, must suffer so that humans will not.

I am getting bigger, wiser and tougher. I have also watched the darker nights with torrential rain. I must apologize mother but you are wrong, there is no wrong in living our life. We must protect our species.

But death is inevitable. - death angel ronin.

Something which is either born or created shall perish one day. All this while, taking little lives, nature has taught me to be gentle. Gentle with death. I don't hold grudges, but still I am the cruelest one. You species love lies that you forget how beautiful the truth is.

I aspire to see the last rain of my life.

You may.

---

i find myself in the same mud again,
where it flows and turns me in ocean red.
i eat the mud, filled with hate,
i puke the sense, like i am never embarrassed.

i find myself in the lake,
which only swallows the men.
the water never touches my will to die,
the deeper it goes, the longer it becomes.

a flame never burned me,
it was a sunrise that i chose voluntarily.

i dared to live with this,
now i seek to end fearlessly!

forbidden garden

my mother named me "blossom",
as she wanted me to bloom,
into the strange world,
which ain't a garden,
yet told me to flourish.

amongst briers,
she forged firm borders,
each flowers and unintentional thorns,
in the garden, that she plant.

forbidding me, the grace she raised,
i chasing the worldly shame,
assuming if this how world runs,
i err, i grew, but life's never been.

maybe i plucked the most redolent floret,
that she cared and hid in her garden.

but what is "blossom",
care, filthy?

a burden, that clogs her breath?
a scent, butchering the garden?

she bedeck her favorite plant with all she had,
water, care, sunshine, love.
and the zeal of cherished vine,
maybe i would never learn to adorn mine.

blue cologne

in brisk yellowish night,
when the street light starts to fade,
the fingertips,
frigid and tremble,
holding arms with blue cologne on.

the bluish shade of this fierce gust,
i would fly!
can i find the blue cologne somewhere else?
i wonder?

like the snow waits,
for the summer, and it melts down.
the teary night waits nothing but,
the ablaze startled from the blue cologne.

she likes the winter,
would rot away within the crisp.
when the wind blows,
it touches each inch of mine skin,
bringing the ocean of that charm,
in every droplet of the blue cologne on.

an epiphany of our long lost touch!

the world never stopped, it would never.
i will hold the last of us, to feel it forever!

i have never been emptier,
now i am an abandoned castle,
i would like to feel the graze of yours,
again, but there's none that i never sought.

i belonged to the woods,
and i kept waiting for the rain to stop,
but now, i am melted in salt.

the touch that one could embrace,
i keep it inside my torn pages,
those slight glances that one must deviate,
tell me, did you still keep looking?

how one could crimp up the stars in their eyes?

why shall i see the sky?
when I could just look in her eyes?

my dear,
the world will hate,
but you hate me in your way,
the world will love,
but you love me in your way.
everything must scrape my soul,
which once belonged to you!

the world will love,
but you love me in your way.
yet i have never been in any way!
all i have is the epiphany of our long lost touch!

death angel ronin

the heaven has never been kinder to me,
for i am, a pretty much of a hell person.
you might regret listening this,
but kindness gets you killed!

the angels' i cannot become,
i might have walked the path of evil,
the fire that i keep in my chest,
tell me, does your heaven claims vicious son?

i will stay right to my wicked layers,
and dance with my demon with his hand on my
waist.
and the heaven which is nice but i plead,
i am no guilt but i have been true to my holy
beings.

let my heart starve, let it burn and crisp out,
the world you built, it's a lie, a hopeless lie.
at least the devil accepts my flaws,
his gentle words, i am everything that i wanna be.

why the angel get to be the best?
does your wings curl up in the grayish sky?
tell me don't you feel tired,
and wanna chop it off?

my lord tells me to bring peace,
what can i say,
i am a work of an imp.
i do not yearn peace,
the soul dies in dusk,
mine's been borrowed and turned scarlet.

angels don't bargain in heaven,
and dead meet in the dorm surreal,
the filthy lies and pretty sins,
swallowed and risked, for a pretty soul.

i'd rather embrace sin and be a sinner,
i'd rather be adorned red and gain possession.
i do not wish to carry fancy wings around my ribs.

i'd tell lies, held upon chest,
tell me if you wanna hear it again.
to the air which strive each part of mine,
i will go down to the earth,
and find the place where i belong.

i adore the demon that i carry within,
and long to be his silken, sweet and seductive sin.
he ignites my soul, what do you know,
i carry the flame within.

---

i carry nothing but agony for myself.

heavy is the burden that I carry,
a weight that's grown and grown and grown,
an agony that gnaws and eats away,
leaving little of me, day by day.

but inside I am shattered and worn,
a soul that's been battered and torn,
by the weight of my own agony,
a darkness that refuses to let me flee.

and so I watch the sun dip below the horizon,
the sky turning from blue to a mandarin,
and as the world hinges on the darkness,
i am left feeling dim, with no divine.

---

with reckless salvation, I make this vow,
to kiss the devil and offer my soul, somehow,
for in the depths of my heart and soul,
i know that only darkness can make me whole.

i'll embrace the flames and dance with the satan,
offering myself, willingly, without a no,
for the price of eternal damnation.

so let the thunder of my veins be heard,
and let the carpet of my blood be your word,
wonder the solace in maze,
find me where it's nothing but rage.

---

beneath the moon's soft glow,
the wolves twirls and sways,
on the fleeting flashes,
that they ingest each night with full grace.

and I, in the solitude of my mind,
watch them dance with awe and delight,
for in her movements, I often find,
a reason to slay, a part of mine.
to be the wolf!

wolves teeth are sharp, like a predator on the hunt,
their tongue licks their lips, with a satisfied grunt,
and as the wolf devours me, with an insatiable glee.

i, a sailor, for the azure

her dark, tangled tresses,
like midnight captive upon her loose hair,
and cosmic ensnare behind those ears.
what does she hold,

a rhythm?
a poetry?
a soul to body?

and the sheer lie, i avoid, blaming beauty.
my eyes can't behold,
like sun's radiant, you mustn't gaze,
but glued in the finesse disguise.

and surge of waves,
that she keeps inside her
black tempestuous eyes,
scorching the sailor,
mi soul that sails.

the longer i sail, the deeper i sink,
once misled, now it's fate'.

what do you call,
one surrenders in depth unknown,
a mystic plunge to felicity?
and the cerulean hunger to be swallowed,
a chase, an enchanting chase?
that i procured.

an ethereal glow in her eyes,
and spatial urge knotted in her hair,
with nothing but everything,
i, a sailor, for the azure.

when traffic light turns into indigo blue

here midnight,
whispers in yellow,
in abbreviated red,
grinning to my face,
the vehicle stops at red,
and depart with green's cue,
i was waiting for the blue blush.

as written in books and guides,
wait for your turn,
then step up on the crossing span.

whom should i follow?
in solitude i tread alone,
no one waits for indigo blue,
no one sees that color anymore.

i shall walk!

what if the vehicle doesn't stop?
what if the crossing line jabs through my stomach?

what if,
it's a lie to wait.
what if i was never meant to pause,
i should have escaped by now.

does indigo blue exist?
do i ever get to leave this town?
or am i lost in a city awry?
here,
chasing flight of an unreal form?

a letter to lord...

why shall i live, my lord?
i shan't breath this lethal,
the heavenly body mustn't dig less,
but one must live gracefully.

i devote the potency, i am his child,
from a womb that he created.
i carry no notion, a blank bare,
a neon light that knows no vintage blush.

a universe that has a start and an end.
twas mystical of me to be born free.
but my majesty,
i stand here,
i carry few questions!

when the waves rises above the skies,
when the beast reaches the golden throne,
when the flower spread venin,
when the earth shed bloody red.
my lord, were you still there?

when the universe was incarnated,
he brought up the cosmic tapestry,
tapped sublimely, an elysian finery.
sprinkled the glitter blemish upon the infinite.

but in this world, humanity born,
acquiesced with immense wisdom,
a human that knows how to love,
a human that kills to feed it's child.
why?

a universe which was born from an art,
he, highly supremely master,
who embodied the rhythmic of fluidity,
where music echoed before a child speak,
a canvas where he sprayed the space.

what shall i say?
we all are a part of your art,
that one must adore.
an art which needs no evolution,
an art that is immortal,
twas mystical of me to be born free.

---

if you go out tonight,
take me with you,
in this chilled night.

when the breeze whips over the sky,
i'd put my palms inside your warm jacket,
like they did in '99.

we'd stop at the gas station,
and we'd buy chips,
that is overly priced.

we'd stare at the moon,
by walking over the wrecked bridge,
we'd talk nonsense till our,
beer cans are emptied,
maybe we'd buy some cheap one,
from the nearest store.

while the street light wanders in night,
we'd wander in the blazing night.
shall we take a ride to another town?

we'd hold the night,
might ponder a bit long in this sight,
if you go out tonight,
take me with you,
in this fiery night.

a salty pond by the edge

in the tender hush of sunday morn',
the pond's embrace, salt-kissed, gently brimming,
beneath the tree's shade, a tranquil sight,
her head on my lap,
as if a wondrous dream stepped into reality.

the serenity unfurled, and time softly stopped.
as laughter echoes, chuckling became louder,
the flowers cascade, petals sway,
a pale white with pinch of lilac like an epilogue.

we wore the same beige shirts,
matching the dress that graces her,
without a blur, she transcends a radiance.

we playfully vie for the song's array,
while i weave a ring,
from the sweet flower bouquet.

dearly pouring the kind of lavender tea,
that she likes,
now it has become a part of mine.

our fingertips graze in delicate caress,
one losing the world, only to gain it all.

an obscure scion in silky closet

the world brighten in blue and pink,
i, born in purple, an obscure scion.
a shiny beacon they gaze in vivid sky,
speak, do you see it too?
or doth drifting in blindness?

if thou raise a child,
whence it speaks, blue or pink,
pray, may i indulge in lilac poetry?
the world fosters-n-nurtures a normal child,
a mí, in shadows veiled, you name it!

closeted...
concealed...
dimmed...?

my mother loves me with all she can,
shall her love persist?
if the verses i speak, that she can't grasp?
may i yet don the purple cloth?
or i shall dive deeper in the pink stain.

a closet i built,
sans wooden frame,
but ordeal wound,
sans brown paint,
but red coursing veins.

tell me if 'tis hour to shatter the closet?
i've been suffocating, merely living!

"you shouldn't be afraid,
the world shatters you in pieces".

but who isn't afraid of death,
must be trembling to live everyday.

the butcher and the beauty

black is i own, like a fairy to the tale,
sublime yet spite, thrown in disgust.

a tranquil space, where worries cease.
and like a cloak, it wraps around.
who holds the beauty and bitterness,
like a shroud, on a deathbed?

the beauty i learnt,
keeping braids,
dying my hair into dark black,
lipstick that i never choose red,
mascara never turned sharp chase.

the beauty my mother own,
like pink on the cherry blossom,
i haze with no pursuit,
lost in a misty trance,
my vision obscured,
as if in a hypnotic dance.

i haze with no pursuit.
but i tend to live in sable.

they colored the black in rosy pink,
a butcher's knife,
dipped in sunken blood.
crimson, hot, red,
then i knew i bled pink.

but what's a monster?

glad you asked,
a monster alike them,
where none sought,
but lie. a soiled lie,
he pretends of human,
draped in deceit's hem.

"a monster" who,
eats the truth away,
with his feisty teeth.
crumbling every piece,
to swallow the sun.

he emerges from the suffocating grief,
he yields his weapon,
with mothers blood.

"but i am no monster",
you live in cunning disguise,
trembling patches,
inking scars.

"look at you, your eyes glows",
agony, but damage they carve.

"my monster" lurks,
stares through my soul,
captive under quilt,
only to inhale when the dusk is gone.

"but what's scarier?",
~a monster or a witch.
they cast away the witches,
witches, who are flames.
threw them to burn.
and created a beast,
for a misguided hunt.

why did the raven stay?

the world on its sharp, slanted edge,
each creature dine in the other,
to see brighter sun.
he had to have made us.
and our survival instinct that,
burns others to light up own town.

raven's are meant for ill luck,
i do not agree.
the world is painted with fake tones,
with false love,
raven's are only thing that speaks truth.

with every spring on the earth,
when the ground turned into dazzling pink,
when the earth saw the hope for better days,
the raven stayed on the hook,
for a death to arrive.

no ravens are seen in a happy place.
have you ever seen any?

when the hope dies, and love loses,
where the creature wins against other one,
raven will stay up late to find their worth.
humans don't stay in the dark,
yet carry a resentment,
while they lack tenderness.

when castles cries in night,
but shines in daylight,
with each canvas hanging,
upon the thin walls of the castle,
the raven know,
how much he can feed himself.

the raven has never been sick,
it never was a disease himself.
yet human afraid to pet him,
they were always afraid,
of someone like them.

golden grave

they dig six feet and a half,
but here i am a - living grave.

wooden, filthy, and confined,
mine had air, a fresh air.

feel like i am stuck within someone,
that i didn't consent to be born in,
the walls within me
smothering and squeezing me,
making me feel numb.

perhaps, a coffin would be
a wiser place,
but looking at myself.
being something
that i don't discern.

carved that skin of mine,
painted it with fair shades,
put my hair in place,
stitched a tag, patched a happy face.

but,
but the air is still grave
- a golden grave.

telling lies each day,
i do, i am, a better woman.
ohh to be a better woman!
tell me,
i should become a woman, first.

injected myself with a heavy ink,
a part of me, a part of that tomb.
put the dusk on, and the label,
here lies *"a better woman".*

how to be a woman?
they said, ask your mother.
only if i could ask,
everything would be much easier.

mother,
your child has always been a deadpan,
part of yours, learnt from you,
maybe someday the lid would open.

i reside in the room with no window,
i breath hollow, i see shadows,
the room is filled with curse,
but no one's more cursed than me.

i reside in a golden grave!

holy november

as the leaves plummeted,
and the bitter gust,
was running through my arms,
sculpting a piece of beam.

ohh holy november.
you left me speechless,
and a part of me illuminating,

i am made of spring,
like the flowers,
bloomed in white-n-pink,
and lanes were painted in immersed wrath.

you are nothing like spring,
the cruelest season in every way possible,
yet i admire to be your child,
we tucked lights up on the wall,
turned november to a burnt orange yet?

with each cold brisk,
like you swallowing of the truth,
and my arms trembling,
trying to hold back the holy november.

flowers on her grave

is it true that,
we cross paths at the dusk?
and we meant to meet again?

is it true that,
i would end up in heaven?
where she has gone?

but no one told me,
she was here,
and everything was a miracle,
nothing less than a heaven.

i'd wait for months,
the feeling of hers in this husky yet zephyr.
i'd feel the raspy october again,
and the hazy touch of hers, again.

those tiny yet sublime and bewitching,
flowers would fall apart,
those white petals with dark amber colored stems.
as we all hoping for her to return.

---

to the wrath and delicacy affection,
where desires are suppressed
chasing a halved love,
left all, and stayed alone.

and the fieriness,
just to be fit among 'em.

a little conceit-n-praising,
of their,
i love it, but they
-imparting to not live in
the chronic-n-typical zone.

if written with the golden ink,
chasing love,
betrayed and disabled.
why turn it into parched pink?

in the abyss despair,
you turned down what a sham love is.

i adore you to be mine holy beings,
where none's been sought,
and get what's been penned.

---

standing atop
corpse heaps.
wildfire of crimson
blood in arm.

the suffering,
aversions of mine.
as i cut my veins
with an axe shine.

i am seeking pain
to kill my another pain,
you can't harm me with words or knife.
i am only responsible for myself.

i am doomed for
hell's service.
this reality is
more hurtful.

i am seeking love
in midst of war!

the axe is my weapon
to kill my deepest sorrow.
sharp sharper!!
it's also wrecking my soul.

whom should i blame
this nation is sinner.
i am no one to claim!!

harm me with your root.
i shall grow up as bugleweed
in that land of deads.

i am sinner
in the
world named
"Sin-ners".

---

didn't we all yearn for
the moon to escape from the murky haze?
only to behold the elegance it possesses.

i wish i were the *moon's favorite child.*

what did the lunar strive?
how does it feel to get cherished by all?
loved by all,
still touched by none.

is this it? what real love is
or merely a fantasy!

the howling of the wolves,
the sacred tongue of worshipers.
a myth or what?

---

trapped in the midst of the red sea
blood splattering across the boat.
sharks in north, storm in west
i came too far, from that dead moat.

I see red as though it is speaking my tale
that deep gulf, better than this cold battle.
lips trembling, fear in the eyes
water you can't take me, i was already eaten alive.

i see a huge boat, packed with woods and humans
"hey miss" come to the boat,
"no" again another sea
stay away my heart screaming with ache
swallow me, i begging to thick air.

i must rot here than going else,
i seek no mercy, come take my bones.
i have read dead poets archives
i'd rather get hit with their stones.

tartar dreams

i did quiver,
when thunder roared at backyard,
asleep in fleeting dreams,
a red cab,
stopped 'neath indigo light
and then a thud.

i trembled in night,
nowhere to snuggle,
or find a solace.
i put blanket on,
as if it will suppress the cries,
it did,
not sound!
but my own fear.

now i am feared enough,
thunder to touch my bones,
part me in pieces.

when i was child,
i didn't know how to run away,
when a snowy shirt,
olive pant,
chased me.

i wanted to hide,
hide in ignorance,
shelter i couldn't find.
so i kept running.

i kept running,
until my school shoes torn apart,
and the dirt ate my feet.
now i no longer run,
i wait for the dirt to fly,
until then i play with it,
feed my mouth with it,
and chew if i was a dirt eater.

a ghostly ghoul

i never saw what a ghost look like?
what his teeth bite like?
how his face darkens,
and his empty eyes glows like?
who are they?

a shadow? vanished in emptiness?
quelled in failure? hidden in dark walls?

i once saw a blurred yet similar face,
his teeth growling like my father's anger did,
i once saw nothing but white eyes,
a deeper cave which could swallow me whole,
no wonder it was a similar,
like i saw in his eyes.

the night is my friend,
so is his. he steps outside,
from all the shallowness.
i feel if it is behind me,
hanging its sorrow on my back.

when the night is dark,
when the moon departs the window span,
i see no one, a cleft chest,
wanting to spill the blood out.

like a mother pats her son, on back,
a ghostly ghoul pats on me.
he is silent,
like a still water in black lake,
the lake knows silence,
only to eat man.

let me in. why not?

i am not braver,
i am not kinder,
i am no human,
i want to drown as a loser child.

when i was a child,
i was afraid of shadows,
i avoided looking under the bed,
behind the doors,
i never opened my cupboard,

the kitchen echoes in pitches,
and calls out my name,
with his smirky face.
his face blurs the night,
and peaking from the window,
that i forgot to close the curtain.
sitting beside me while i sleep,
it stares in my eyes, as if i awe him
my man, how foolish i am.
it has swallowed me,
now its all over my mind.

i afraid, a child talks about god,
i talk about demons,
but demon danced with me,
when i was alone on the stage.

i do not carry love,
or affection for living,
i am filled with hatred,
grudges as my man taught me to be.

i kept running from the shadows,
i forgot it was a black silken carpet i was running on.

hazel

i recalled the rusty eve,
an artistry graced my sight.
a celestial advent she had.
as she lingered, and bell did tinkle
the sound synced with mine heartbeat,
three beats skipped, and caught at fourth.

as she appeared the café's threshold,
her silhouette profound,
a fleeting flash, did i embrace?

kind of rusty brown and wine like burgundy shade
she put in her hair.
her hazel eyes, lucent to the setting noon's kiss,
glowing back, dancing in harmony,
one could see the eminent she kept.

the apricot striped coat,
along with the beige shirt,
and a butterfly around the neck chain she had.
my my, as if the aphrodite graced the earth air.

she sauntered past the gate,
paused for a bit.
and her honeyed oud scent wafted,
maybe i'd spend all days, to seek this one.

HAZEL,
like poetry has carved her name.
she sat around the corner,
only if i could see the tapestry.

she drew out one of her books,
that seemed a little older and wiser,
she clasped the cover,
the sage green nail gleamed impeccable.

some torn pages, with ink sprayed,
maybe she bid notes to remember,
dipped in barn red that dead floret fell,
a crumbling chime,
maybe her lover gave and she put ahead the cover.

like an irish coffee she sipped,
drunk on the sweet perfume,
tell me to abide,
but i shall write a poem.

i looked up,
maybe she disappeared in thin air,
like a magic leaves you hinged, stunned for a bit.
was it truly a magic?
or a dream i'd be dreaming?

---

what's heavier?
a soul crying out loud to be heard,
a loneliness thumping upon your chest,
a heart seeking to be melt,
or a crushing grasp of hollowness.

are we not fated for happiness?
but what is happiness?
a five year old child, feels joy
- when he sees his new favorite toy.
but what should i do?
why i should keep making them happy,
when it only makes me even sadder.

About the Author

Greetings, from Arvina Kori, though you're welcome to address her as "Arko"; By daylight, she specializes in the art of overthinking, and in night, she transforms into an amateur poet, chasing the moon's muse with humble and some offensive words. Great at listening, worst at making coffees. Also she spends her entire day listening to 2-5 songs and scrolling when she got work to do.

Writer's Pocket

Writer's Pocket is a publication house established in 2016. We began with the aim of providing a better publishing platform for aspiring writers and budding poets.

The publishing industry in India (and around the world, to a great extent) is always something of a mystery even to the writers themselves. We are working on making publishing more accessible to everyone.

So far, we have helped over 3,000 writers turn their dreams into reality by publishing the books and continue to do so. By doing so, we also provide some of the best content by Indian writers to the readers.

Want to read more books? Scan this QR code with your smartphone and check out all our books on Amazon.